WOMEN FOOD AND GOD
COLORING BOOK

GENEEN ROTH

SCRIBNER

New York   London   Toronto   Sydney   New Delhi

SCRIBNER
An Imprint of Simon & Schuster, Inc.
1230 Avenue of the Americas
New York, NY 10020

First Scribner paperback edition November 2016

SCRIBNER and design are registered trademarks of The Gale Group, Inc.,
used under license by Simon & Schuster, Inc., the publisher of this work.

For information about special discounts for bulk purchases,
please contact Simon & Schuster Special Sales at 1-866-506-1949
or business@simonandschuster.com.

The Simon & Schuster Speakers Bureau can bring authors to your live event.
For more information or to book an event, contact the Simon & Schuster Speakers Bureau at
1-866-248-3049 or visit our website at www.simonspeakers.com.

Interior design by Erich Hobbing

Manufactured in the United States of America

3   5   7   9   10   8   6   4   2

Library of Congress Cataloging-in-Publication Data is available.

ISBN 978-1-5011-6191-9

All illustrations © Shutterstock.

Introduction

When I think of coloring, I think of *Romper Room* (a children's television show) and the day that Miss Mary Ann held up the rose I'd spent hours coloring. I was two years old and I still remember that orange-green-purple rose, and the thrill of opening a box of Crayola crayons and being able to choose any color I wanted. Having a drawing in front of me felt like being given a chance to become anything, everything, through color.

I'd forgotten about creating a world through coloring until recently (although I have never forgiven Miss Mary Ann for not mentioning my name when she held up my rose; there is a chance I hold on to grudges a half century longer than necessary), partly because I'd assumed that coloring was for little kids, not big kids like you or me. Now suddenly, with the surge of adult coloring books, the invitation to be transported into a vivid world by creating a feast of color is here again.

My friend Barbara once told me that "what other people consider necessity, I consider irrelevant. What I consider necessity, they consider luxury." As I listened to her, I realized that it's possible to reframe the immersion into beauty and color as a necessity, not a luxury. Creating and then feasting on gorgeousness is nourishing. Lavishing yourself with color is calming. Stopping the endless daily litany of bad news, what's wrong and who's to blame is a necessity if we want to remain sane and balanced. Also—this is important—it's fun.

In this book, I've paired my favorite lines from *Women Food and God* with illustrations that evoke their meanings. After you read the quotes, it might be helpful to allow them to affect you without thinking too much. Discover where and how they touch you. Let beauty and color take you on their wings. Allow yourself to soar.

My hope is that you decide that you are worth giving yourself time to leaf through the pages, read the quotes, and color one enchanting image after another. And that in the process, you remember your inherent loveliness. Because after all, the gorgeousness you create on these pages, as saturated as they may be, is only a pale reflection of who and what you already are. Remembering that is the true necessity.

WOMEN FOOD
AND GOD
COLORING BOOK

Compulsive eating
is a psychological and physical challenge,
but it is also a doorway
into a dazzling inner universe.

Everything we believe about love, fear, transformation and God is revealed in how, when and what we eat.

God is not just in the details;
God is also in the muffins,
the fried sweet potatoes
and the tomato vegetable soup. God—
however we define him or her—
is on our plates.

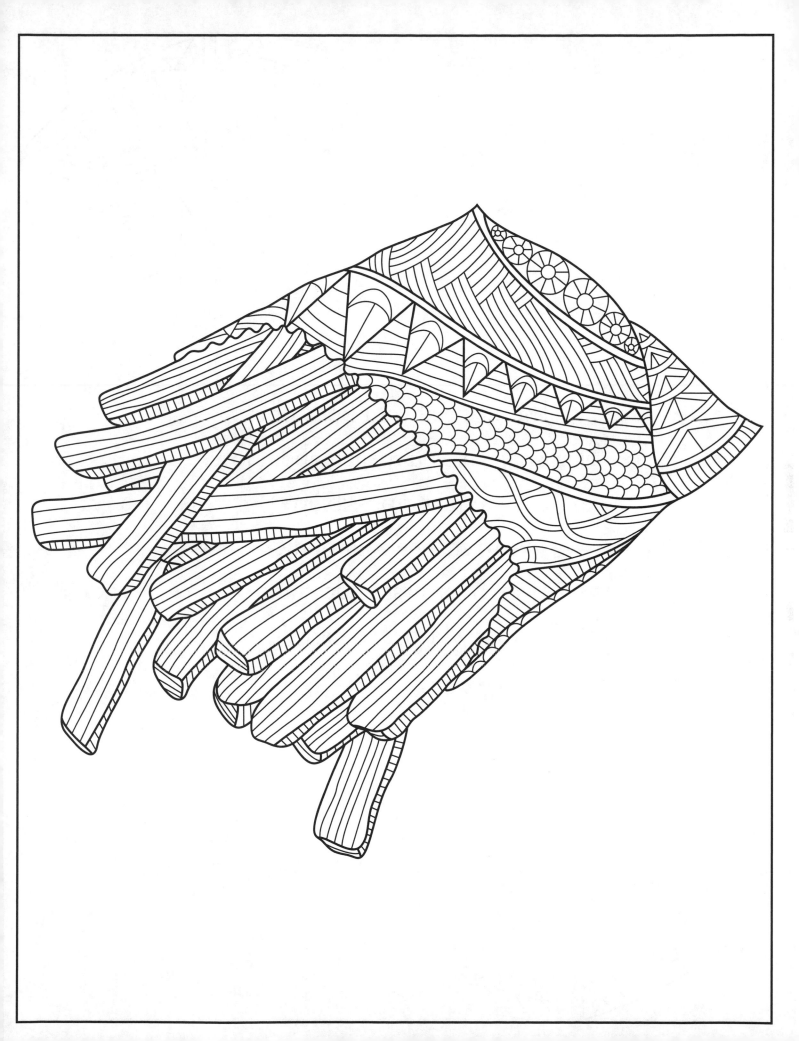

The shape of your body obeys
the shape of your beliefs about love,
value and possibility.
To change your body,
you must first understand
that which is shaping it.

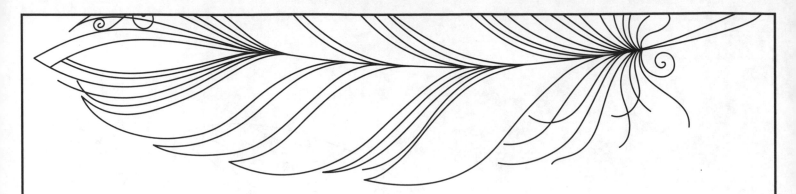

I turned to food for the same reasons
that people turned to God: it was my sigh of ecstasy,
my transport to heaven, my concrete proof that relief
from the pain of everyday life was possible.

When you no longer believe that eating will save your life when you feel exhausted or overwhelmed or lonely, you will stop.

When you take care of yourself with food,
it becomes apparent that eating
is only about one thing:
nourishing your body.
And it wants to soar.

Women turn to food when they are not hungry
because they *are* hungry for something they can't name:
a connection to what is beyond the concerns of daily life.
Something deathless, something sacred.

Relentless attempts to be thin take you
further and further away from what could actually
end your suffering: getting back in touch
with who you really are.

You are not a mistake.

You are not a problem to be solved.

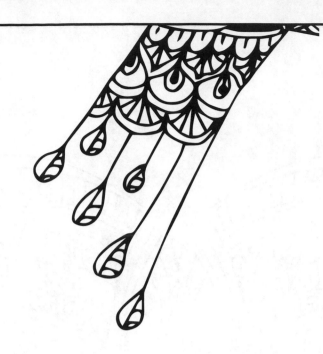

Obsession gives you something to do
besides having your heart shattered
by heart-shattering events.

There is a whole universe to discover
between "I'm feeling empty"
and turning to food to make
the emptiness go away.

There are worse things in life
than a broken heart.

Imagine not being frightened by any feeling.
Imagine knowing that nothing will destroy you.
That you are beyond any feeling, any state.
Bigger than. Vaster than.

Our lack of acceptance
about the way things/we are
and our unhappiness are
exactly synonymous.

When you stop and let yourself feel
what is being offered to you,
it is never, ever what you thought it would be.
You go from being afraid to being
a fountain in three minutes.

What if what you needed was right in front of you but you kept missing it because you were looking for something else?

Brokenness is learned, not innate.
Our work is to find our way back
to what is already whole.

If you focus on getting the dishes done
so that your kitchen will be clean,
you miss everything that happens between dirty and clean.
The warmth of the water, the pop of the bubbles,
the movements of your hand. You miss the life that happens
in the middle zone—between now and what you think
your life should be like.

Diets are based on the unspoken fear
that you are a madwoman,
a food terrorist, a lunatic.

Spiritual hunger can never be solved
on the physical level.

Our work is not to change what you do,
but to witness what you do with enough awareness,
curiosity and tenderness that the lies and old decisions
upon which the compulsion is based
become apparent and fall away.

When the shape of your body
no longer matches the shape of your beliefs,
the weight disappears.

Everything we do, I tell my students,
is to reteach ourselves
our loveliness.

Goodness and loveliness are possible,
even in something as mundane
as what you put in your mouth for breakfast.
Beginning now.

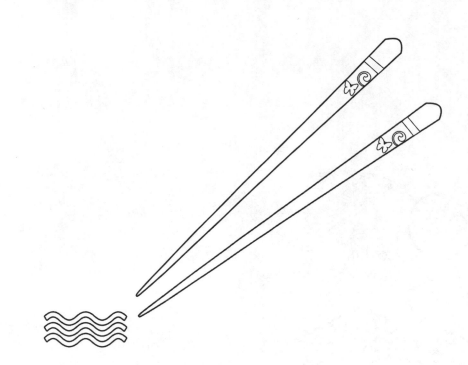

No matter how developed you are
in any other area of your life,
no matter what you say you believe,
no matter how sophisticated or enlightened
you think you are, how you eat tells all.

Awareness is the ability to know
what you are feeling.
Presence is the ability to inhabit
a feeling while sensing that which
is bigger than the feeling.

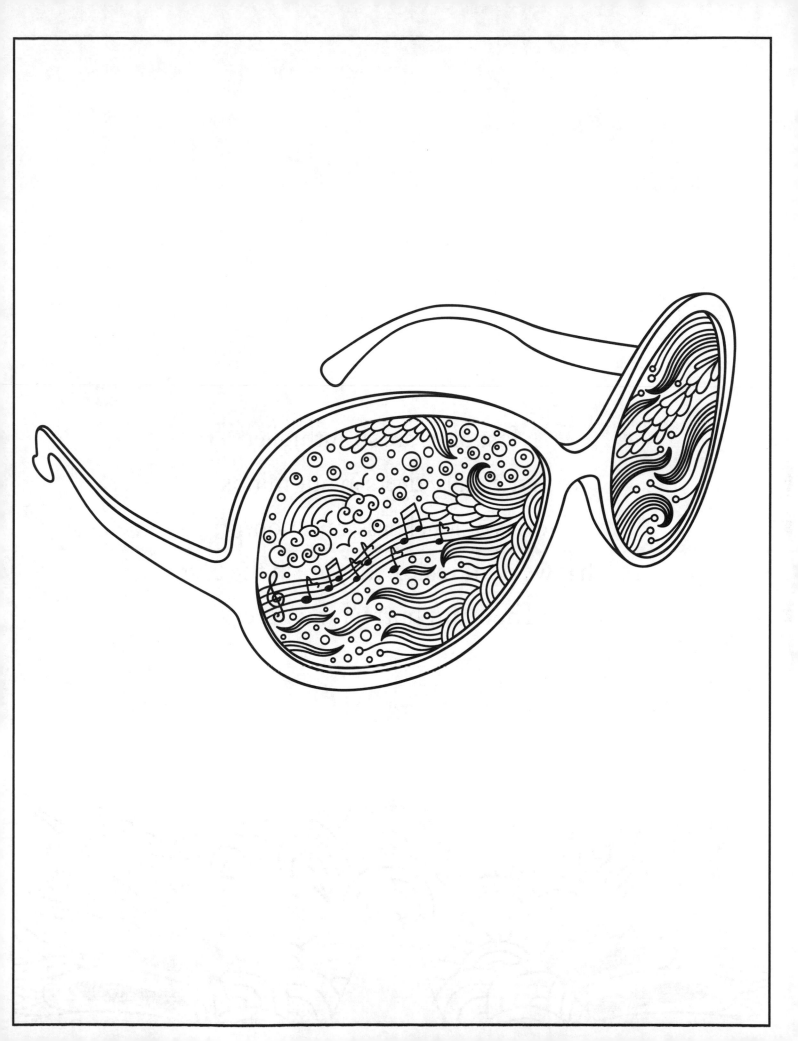

Most of us are so enthralled
with the scary tigers in our minds—
our stories of loneliness, rejection, grief—
that we don't realize they are in the past.
They can't hurt us anymore.

All any feeling wants
is to be welcomed with tenderness.
It wants to dissolve like a thousand writhing snakes
that with a flick of kindness become harmless
strands of rope.

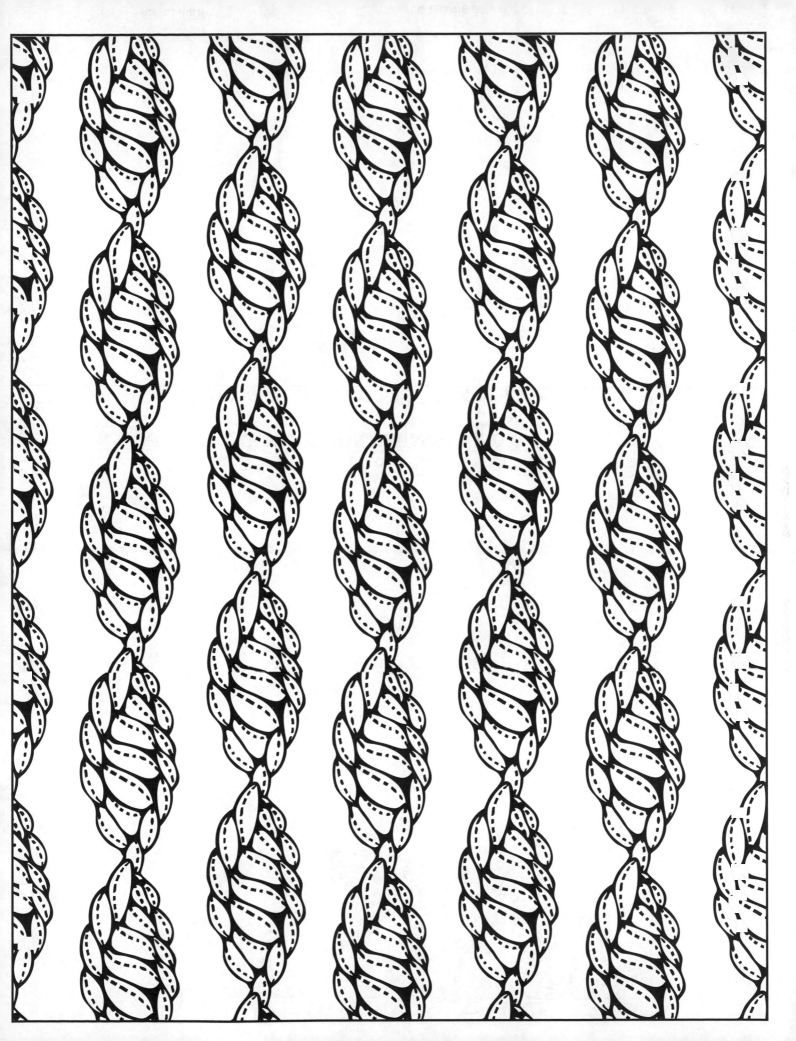

We avoid feelings because of the story
we tell ourselves about them.

Meditation helps you discover what you love
that you didn't know you loved
because you were so caught up in your mind
that you didn't realize anything else was there.

Obsession is a way
of organizing our lives
so that we never have to deal
with the hard part—
the part that happens
between being two years old
and dying.

The problem isn't that we have bodies;
the problem is that we're not living in them.
Sigh.

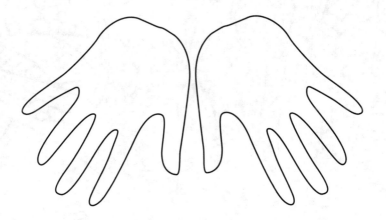

Your body is the piece of the universe
you've been given.

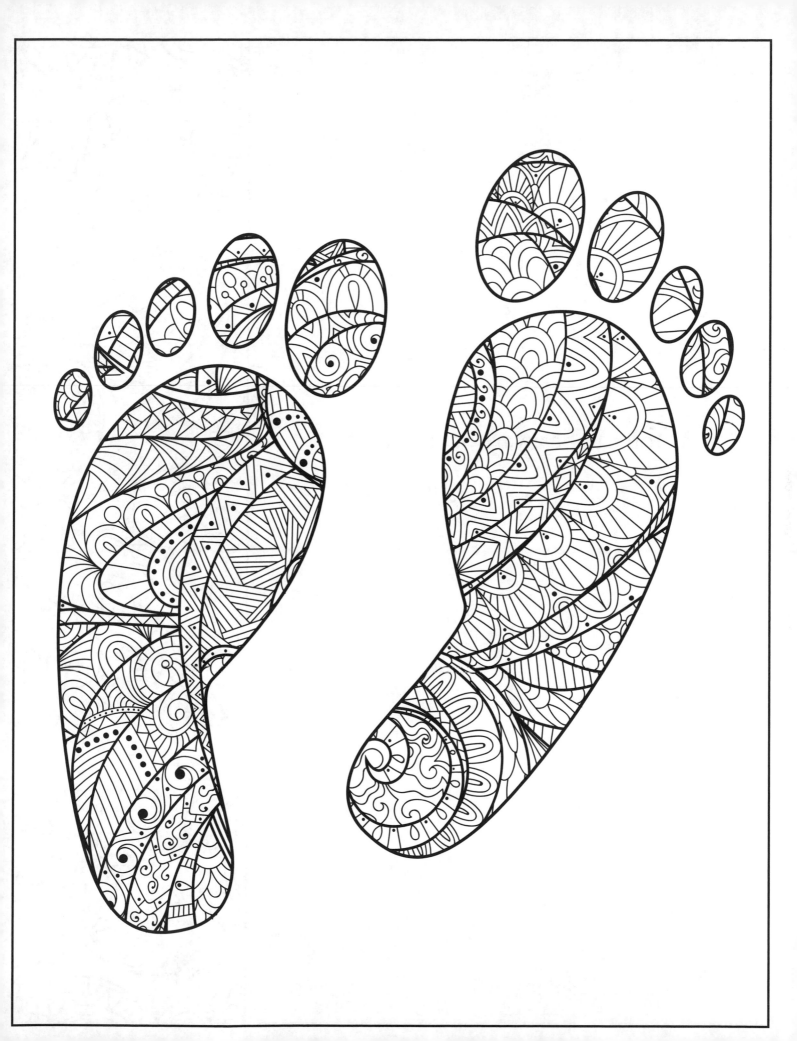

You can be aware of your past
without being it.

I thought that if I let myself
eat what I couldn't eat as a kid,
I could get what I never got.

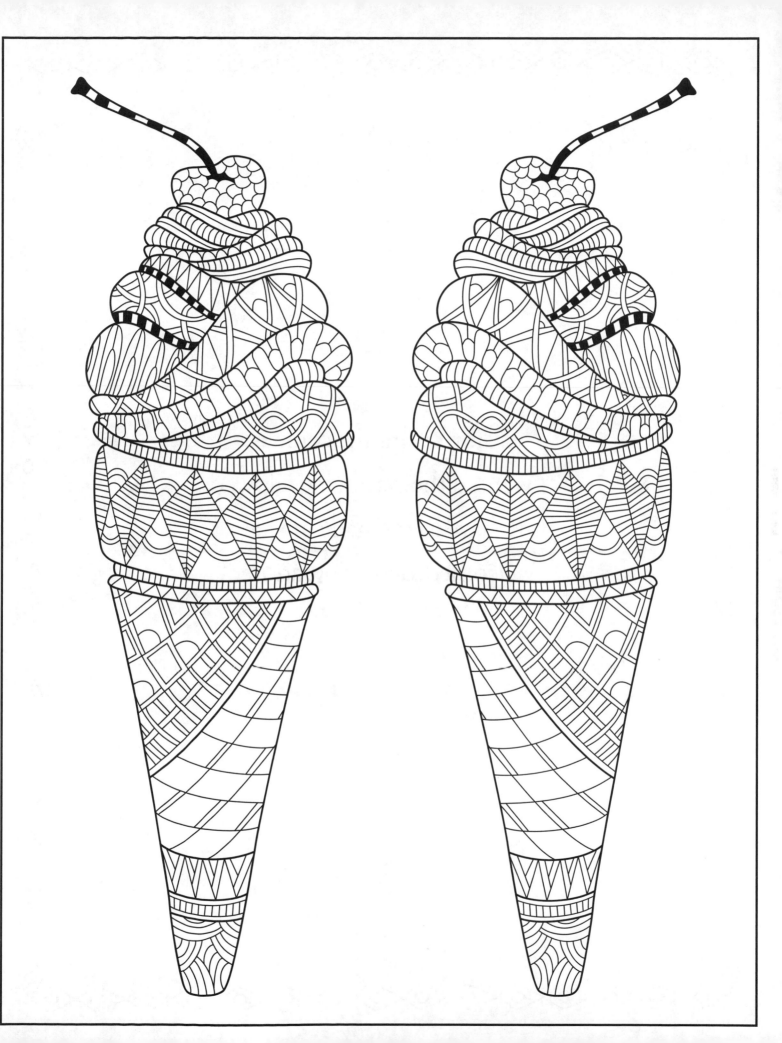

I didn't want the cookies;
I wanted the way being allowed
to have them made me feel:
welcomed, deserving, adored.

Although the very notion that hatred
leads to love and that torture
leads to relaxation is absolutely insane,
we hypnotize ourselves into believing
that the end justifies the means.

It's never been true,
not anywhere at any time,
that the value of a soul,
of a human spirit,
is dependent on a number
on a scale.

Come break the trance.
Pay attention to your breath.
Your arms. Your legs.
Wake up to the riot of life
around you every second.

We don't want to *eat* hot fudge sundaes
as much as we want our lives
to *be* hot fudge sundaes.

When you pay attention to yourself,
you notice the difference
between being tired and being hungry.
Between being satisfied and being full.
Between wanting to scream
and wanting to eat.

The purpose of a spiritual path or religion
is to provide a precise and believable way
into what seems unbelievable.

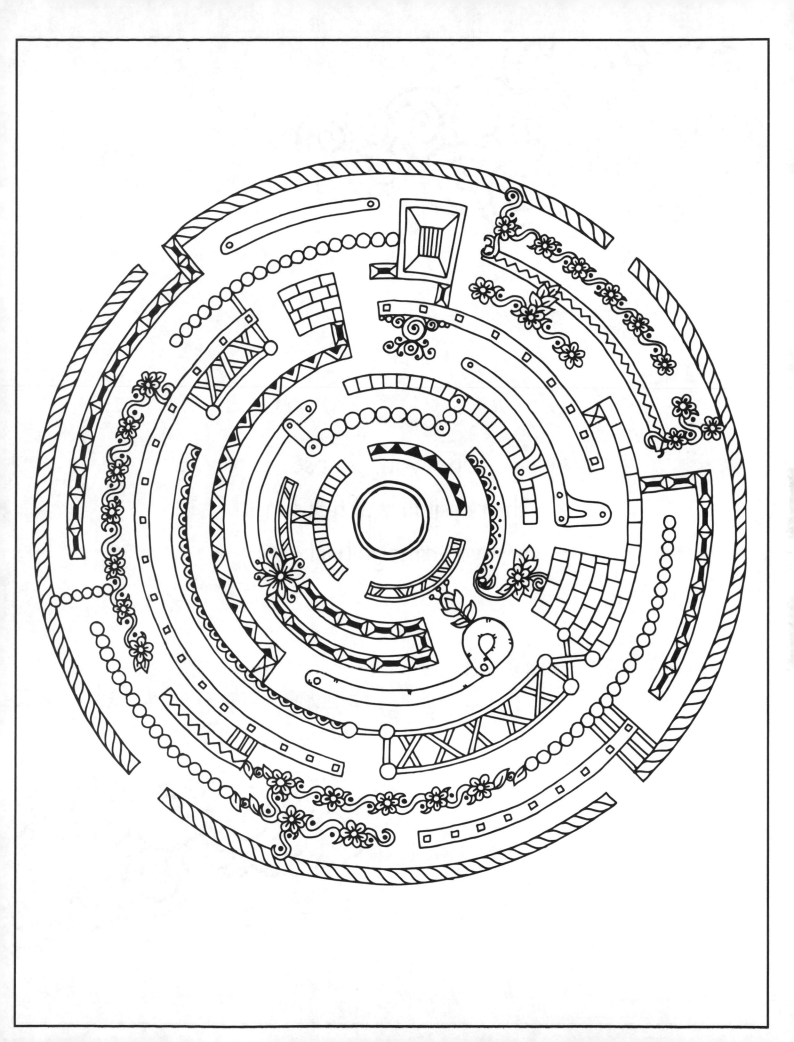

Once you glimpse
the possibility of freedom,
you can't go back.